Freedom
Behind Bars

Testimonies of Faith

Kimberly Bethann Fincher

ISBN-10: 1463677286
ISBN-13: 978-1463677282

DEDICATION

This book is dedicated to all my Brothers and Sisters
in prison and our Heavenly Father whose grace and mercy
has set us free.

CONTENTS

ACKNOWLEDGMENTS

Thank you to all my Brothers and Sisters who were brave enough to share their stories of struggles and faith behind bars. We may never meet, but once you accept Jesus Christ; we become family for eternity. To my husband whose love and compassion encourages me to move forward each day. To our Pastor Gary Johnson, whose ministry keeps us lifted and encouraged in God's Word. To the many members of Calvary Worship Center who have showed my family the Love of Jesus Christ.

1 ALFONSO HERNANDEZ

The earliest letters I have from Alfonso are from 11-03-10 until 01-19-10 he told his story a little bit in each letter so I'm going to attempt to put together the story from each letter and I hope that he will send me the rest of the story as I'm writing this.

My Encounters with Jesus Christ:
 How He Saved Me Many Times from Death and Life Sentences in Prison

I remember mom would always take me and my sisters and brother to church every Sunday, to try and obliterate all the negative actions that took place in our household, (having to live with an abusive father, changed every single one of us). I recall listening to mom crying in her room, from her anguish; wanting to escape all the unhappy moments. I would always hug mom and whisper in her ear that, "I love you, everything will be ok." I was only 5-6 years old at the time. It was around that age when I started having a little knowledge of God.

Jumping from denomination to denomination, made us land in a small house-like church in Chaparral, New Mexico. That's where I saw the love and work of Jesus Christ through all the loving believers. The change did not occur then and there. I was still a brat, but I was grateful for having food, a home, and a loving mother. I also knew that as long as Jesus Christ was around there would always be hope.

Our father use to hold us hostage with kitchen knives, intoxicated and furious. Let me rewind to where I left off last letter. There was a time when Dad realized he was being abusive towards his family, so he started attending church with us. I was ecstatic knowing dad was changing. He started taking us camping twice a month to New Mexico. I was 11-12 years old at the time. I was already sneaking out, every chance I had to smoke. My older sister would watch me, and throw parties. The older guys would get me drunk and laugh at me acting up. I was a kid and didn't know how to act, especially drunk at 11. There were times when dad would have his down falls and they weren't nice. I started being rebellious towards society at age 13; smoking weed and drinking cheap beer. Anything that would keep me away from the reality that was going on around me. Mother was trying so hard to be a good Mom to us, but sometimes I could detect sadness in her face. She started taking us to this church in Juarez, Chiuh-Mexico; across the border. Her sisters were Christians living there. I'm telling you, this was a nice church; with the friendliest people on the planet! At this time of my life, I can actually say was the happiest; getting to know Jesus Christ through all the people that were there. I love the band, the bible studies, the walks on the park, passing out Christian literature, and talking to them about our Savior. The whole church would go camping together!

We would make great bonfires and praise the Lord. I even had me a nice Christian girlfriend. I never wanted to go back to El Paso. We were all doing good! Even Dad. I remember when the Pastor would say, "Is there anyone in here that would like to give his or her life to God?" I always sat at the back, almost hidden from everyone. One Sunday morning, as Pastor was saying this everyone stood and the music was playing in the background; while people were surrendering their lives to God; I had my head down, because we were in prayer. I heard the Pastor say, "You, on the back." I didn't know who he was talking to, so I looked up and his eyes were set on me. He told me, "Yes you, come on down." I hesitated for a while, because you usually raise your hand to be converted into a new child. So, I looked around, and everyone was gesturing for me to go, so I did! It was awesome, my body felt light. I started to cry without being bashful. I was 13 years old, almost 14, getting ready for high school. I knew that I couldn't use drugs nor degenerate the temple of God anymore. I knew I needed to stay focused and positive. Having to live in a different country, and go to church in a different country was going to be hard. The journey I took from there became bumpy. The light started fading away, until it was total darkness. I lost myself in the devils playground. When my family and I stopped going to church, and I was entering high school, my life just flipped! I went from going to church and trying to stay on the right path to playing football and going head on with a 200 pound line man, without a helmet. I was drinking and smoking pot every day and skipping classes. When I did go to class, I was the bad boy; with dark shades, and always being belligerent towards the teachers. I was as destructive as they can get. From burning down a class room, graffiti on the walls, being shot at several times during lunch hour. I started out on

3

weed and went on to acid to cocaine. You would find me in the darkest and most dangerous places in Juarez, Mexico; just to score some drugs. I've had friends die from drug overdoses, being shot to death and getting into fatal car wrecks. I've been in several wrecks with not a single scratch. Around this time me and my youngest sister were the only ones left staying at our parents' house. The rest got married, or moved out with someone; not wanting to deal with our fathers fury. Our father was still a good working man, but when he would drink you wouldn't want to be near him. I remember one day I was out partying with a girlfriend of mine, (she became my wife, but that's another story). She received a call from one of my sisters, saying that my little sister was able to place a call; that she was scared and crying because dad had her and mom trapped inside the house with a knife; threatening to kill them if they left. When I arrived at our home, it was surrounded by cops. I was scared thinking that he did something to them. I acted out before thinking, running into the house and struggling with dad; until I had him in a good hold, then the cops came barging in. At this point of my life I was fed up. So, I stopped hanging around the bad crowds and got married, thinking my life would change for the better. My life just got worse!

I recently received a letter from Alfonso and he said that he was struggling with his faith and was doing some wrong things. He said that he would get back on the right track though and wasn't going to give up serving God.

2 ARMANDO DELACRUZ

"Arise, shine; for your light has come! And then the Glory of the Lord is risen upon you." Isaiah 60:1 NIV

Greetings to you, your family and your prophetic future in Jesus' name!

Beloved, I received your most welcome letter 2 weeks ago. Therefore, allow me to present to you this letter on my behalf with a heart of gratitude; as we have briefly shared knowledge about God's Holy word. Though, I also present this letter in a state of concern, obligation and with compassion. Because, as I read your letter; I frowned and groaned within as disappointment covered me from head to toe.

I knew within my spirit that you choosing to stop all personal communication with us, who are behind bars; may happen soon. This was one reason why I was hesitant in writing, when I first read about you all in the Free Life Newsletter and why I didn't come straight and to the point about all going on in my life. You sounded a great trumpet to the captives when you offered to help and encourage us. I knew your offer was genuine, but I also knew that the response of the multitude would be too great.

God's word reveals this to be so in Matthew 9:37-38. But, in your letter you clearly specified you would forward our letters to other members of your church; so then I assumed you were alert, focused and well prepared.

But, this may not have been so. So, if so please allow me to sincerely apologize and say I am sorry if I caused more weight or burden to your life. So, as Job once said I also say, Job 1:21b *"The Lord gave and the Lord has taken away; Blessed be the name of the Lord."*

I pray that all your decisions have been Holy Spirit inspired and so by inquired and made in God's Holy presence. I also hope you are now divinely settled in your God given geographical destination. For it's unsafe to be unstable, for these situations create a doorway for satan to gain entry into our lives and ministries. What has happened? Why a change of heart and route? I feel so disappointed because you are the 2nd type of minister and perhaps the 3rd on the way as we speak, that offers friendship, hope and encouragement and then to say all of a sudden, that other obligations have come up. Lord have mercy! For this shows a lack of discipline and commitment. The Jesus I know and serve would never, EVER abandon and decline from His ministry and sheep. Matth. 9:35-38, especially when the pressure came- He groaned and was bold and aggressive: Matth. 14:9-21, Luke 4:18-19,43; 9:22; 10:19; 12:33,35; 16:16. The God I now know and serve is always the same yesterday, tomorrow and for eternity. He's not man that relents or changes His mind. Numb. 23:19, 1 Sam. 15:29. He is a God that highly equips us from head to toe and directs our every step, but only if we seek first and only His glory and Kingdom. Matth. 6:33. And for every good work: Eph. 4:11-12; 2 Tim. 3:16-17, Prov. 4:26; 10:8; 16:9.

Is this not the same God you serve???

My sweet and dear Sister Kim, by no means am I trying to tear you down and chop your head off, or any type of offense. God forbid, and have Mercy! Luke 17:1 it's impossible that no offense comes, but woe (curse) to him through whom they do come! May God deal with me if I speak here today anything less than scriptural truth. For, this is part of His teachings that I am sharing and many times truth hurts. But, nevertheless truth if received and put to work will set us free. John 8:31-32, 36 and furthermore, it creates in us a living Holy testimony; as you are well known and which brings to pass Rev. 12:12!

I am greatly concerned for your service to God. It is both better to be in the wilderness with God's Holy presence and labor with unpleasant people, than to go to the "Promise Land" where it's more peaceful and comfortable and less hassle, but God's presence is nowhere around. Read Moses encounter: Exodus 32:27-34:14...

You seem to be like Jonah, like not full throttle but stray and declining into another route, that is not rooted in the belly of your heart. John 7:38

I remember I once didn't understand a statement that you made in one of your previous letters, so I asked you what you meant and your purpose for such a statement. (yes the statement was about your moma didn't get u in prison) Well, your reply was bold and quite strong and very well said. Around that time I also mentioned to you that you seem to be tough as nails, but I also was strong like Iron...Your reply was for me to wake up and get real!

For this is exactly what you are about: being real with us, so that we can get real with God. Because, we inmates tend to fool ourselves into thinking that we don't have any problems and therefore we seek no real effort in making changes. Also, that you will always minister to the captives because; this is your life. I know your strong and as tough as nails and that your desire is genuine, honest and sincere; for it clearly shows. But, this type of choice shows otherwise and does not follow biblical truth. Gods word teaches us to plant and water His seeds, to take possession of the land, to utterly destroy the enemy within ourselves and upon the land; to be strong, multiply and fruitful there and everywhere. Deut. 10:11-14:2

So, stand up, arise and take up your position and make satan flee. Fight, fight sister. For I know the Power and Blood of Jesus runs through your veins. Let the Holy Spirit cover you with His compassion and ignite a Holy fire carnival within you that not even satan can put out. God's word reveals in Isaiah 59:19b, that the Spirit of the Lord will lift up and standard against satan; when the flood comes in. I will be within that standard, how about you? He will also renew our strength, that we mount up with wings like eagles and so we will run and not be weary, we shall walk and not faint. Isaiah 39:31 and let us not forget Mark 16:15-18; Luke 10:18-20. But, let us not be deceived that life will be peaches and cream, because Jesus Himself said that trouble will come, if they hated me; they will hate you; if they persecuted me, they will persecute you. But, this is where the line is drawn, as it was in the desert and where winners and losers and sheep and goats are separated; as we walk with the spirit of discernment. Because, both of us must be very well aware that it takes commitment, sound mind, power, and love, compassion and God's Glory to minister to the captives; and to decline any step or half a step backwards IS NOT AN OPTION!!

Furthermore, we should know that we seek and need special and necessary attention that demands a close fellowship. I know the Holy Spirit Himself has spoken here today, so please heed it's words the Lord Jesus Christ said to Peter 3 times in John 21:14-17, "Do you love Me? Then feed my sheep!" God only expects from us to do what He has only equipped us to do. So, if you have been called and God has bestowed on you the gift of Life, the ability and power; use it mightily and very wisely. Luke 19:11-27

Beloved, I pray that you receive these words with favor and may the Lord grant you peace in your mind and guard your heart. I hope and pray this will not be the end, but the beginning of a greater and stronger journey. I will be expecting an answer from the address you once sent me which was a Christian college half-way house called Calvary

Commission. I sent the application the day after resurrection day, meaning Easter. I am waiting for a response from the perhaps within 2 weeks; to see if I will be accepted and be able to parole there on my parole date September 2011, coming up soon. If accepted perhaps we may be able to meet some day. But, all in God's will and time.

Well, allow me to close this long letter for I did not intend to write this long; so I will close because I know you have other important matters. May God Bless and may you have great days ahead of you and with these in thought I say good-bye. 1 Peter 4:7 the end of all things is at hand, therefore be serious and watchful in your prayers...

"A Student in Christ"

   A. Dela Cruz Jr.

"At one period of time I was convinced that I could no longer write to inmates and be a mom and wife too. God showed me otherwise and I continue the good fight of encouraging God's precious children behind bars. I received Armando's letter of encouragement with great appreciation and respect as my Brother in Christ it was a word from God. The road of a minister and servant of God is lonely and long but not without joy and reward." Kim B. Fincher

3 CHRIS SMITH

The Foundation of Unity

It was once said, "United we stand, divided we fall." Psalm 133:1,3 says, *"How wonderful and pleasant it is when brothers live together in harmony! Harmony is as refreshing as the dew from Mount Hermon that falls on the mountains of Zion. And there the Lord has pronounced His blessing, even life everlasting."* (NLT) If we live together in harmony, with our brothers and sisters, God has promised that He will bless us! Unity is one of the most important qualities that the body of Christ should exhibit. The foundation of unity in Christ is love. Romans 5:8 says, *"But God put His love on the line for us, by offering His Son in sacrificial death while we were of no use whatsoever to Him."* (MSG)

This is the unconditional love or agape love of our Father God for us through Christ Jesus. This is the kind of love that we are to show others, including those that hurt us, and especially those that are a part of the body of Christ. Most of the time, we judge and ridicule each other; instead of loving each other.

We should take a moment to ask: What would Jesus do? And then we would laugh at our childish behavior. God sees everything we do and knows our hearts. What would we do differently if we thought about this fact before making a move?

Romans 14:4 says, *"Who are you to condemn someone else's servants? They are responsible to the Lord, so let Him judge whether they are right or wrong. And with the Lord's help, they will do what is right and will receive His approval."* (NLT) Romans 14:10, *"So, why do you condemn another believer? Why do you look down on another believer? Remember, we will all stand before the judgment seat of God."*

Unconditional love says, "I'll die for you even though you reject me. I'll die for you although you spit in my face, or slap me, or beat me, or torture me, or do anything at all to me, no matter what." This is Christ-like love and what Jesus did for us! *"If anyone boasts, "I love God," and goes right on hating his brother or sister, thinking nothing of it, he is a liar. If he won't love the person he can see, how can he love the God he can't see? The command we have from Christ is blunt: Loving God includes loving people. You've got to love both." 1 John 4:20-21(MSG)*

Why is it so hard for us to show unconditional love? When someone hurts us: emotionally, mentally, physically, or spiritually; it creates a wound in us. We tend to carry this wound with us and if we don't allow God's word and love to heal it, the wound will fester and become infected. We must seek God's help and lay our burdens and wounds on His Cross to heal.

We need to pray to Him: *"Father God, please help me heal this offense, this wound. I need help forgiving this person who hurt me. Lord, I need your Holy Spirit, your agape love to dwell inside of me. And help me show the love of Christ Jesus to the one who hurt me. Amen"* *"Delight yourselves in the Lord and He will give you the desires of your heart."* Psalms 37:4 *"So then, let us aim for harmony in the church, and try to build each other up."* Romans 14:19

"You were all created to travel on the same road, and in the same direction, so stay together, both outwardly and inwardly. You have; one Master, one faith, one baptism, one God, and Father of all, who rules over all, works through all, and is present in all. Everything you are and think and do is permeated with oneness." (MSG)

So we should be humble, gentle, loving, patient, and peaceful and deny ourselves. We need to get over ourselves; and put God where He belongs-First.

> *"This is how I want you to conduct yourself in these matters. If you enter your place of worship and, about to make an offering, you suddenly remember a grudge a friend has against you, abandon your offering, leave immediately, go to this friend and make things right. Then and only then, come back and work things out with God."*
Matthew 5:23-24

Our relationship with God will be hindered until we work out our differences with others. When we accept freedom through Jesus Christ we are made new in His image; but we still have a choice and sometimes choose to rebel and get caught up in self. We miss out on all that God has set for us on the table of Salvation when we try to do it our own way. When we walk in the faith of our salvation we are blessed by God's loving Grace. Jesus is our example of how we are to live. He was God in the physical form. He did not sin, although tempted as we are.

I am so glad that in spite of my faults, fears, failures, and frailties that He didn't forsake me or you. In spite of the sins we have committed, He saved us! Although Jesus stumbled under the weight of the Cross going up the hill of Calvary He didn't drop and leave it. Jesus carried the burdens of our sins on that Cross! He chose to show us He loves us more than anything else. He surrendered all for us. So, we don't have to carry all those burdens of sin in us or on us. We can lay them down on the Cross! He gave us the perfect example to live by. His unconditional love for all of mankind is what kept Him hanging on the cross in agony and pain, until IT WAS FINISHED. Although He died, He also rose, so that we might have life, life to the fullest and even life everlasting in Him.

In unity with the Apostle Paul when he addressed the church in Corinth, *"I appeal to you, dear brothers and sisters, because you belong to Jesus, to live in harmony with each other. Let there be no divisions in the church. Rather, be of one mind, united in thought, and purpose."* 1 Corinthians 1:10

14 DARYL HESS

Dear Kim, I pray this letter finds you well in health and spirit, my name is Daryl Hess and I'm in prison in Oklahoma. I am a new believer in Christ. I have confessed my sins, asked for forgiveness and gave my life to God! I'm working my way through the bible for the first time in my life. I turned 30 this last Oct. 16th. I have what I now believe a powerful testimony, and a prime example of God's love and why Jesus died for us. Rather than just a past full of sin. I am doing a total of 56 years in prison. I may very well never get out. But, I have unwavering faith that God has a plan for my life. I don't know what it is yet, and i don't have much time to fulfill it; but my heart, eyes and ears are open.

I hit bottom in 2007, with a major drug habit and committed armed robberies. Things were bad and once I sobered up in jail I realized it. Yet, I still continued to live in sin; until recently. I am now on protective custody. There is a group within this system that has tried; and will try again if given the opportunity, to murder me. They are called the Universal Aryan Brotherhood. I don't know where you have done time, but maybe you know of them. I found myself counting my last minutes of life; strapped to a stretcher, and I prayed for the first time since I was 8 or 9. I said, "*God, I've done alot of wrong, ignored you, I doubt I'll see heaven, but Lord, I'm sorry. Please forgive me and be with me until the end. I need you!*" Oddly, I felt very little pain then. I realize now that it was God helping me, holding my hand during the most difficult and traumatic time of my life. God pulled me through! I haven't reached my end on this earth yet and God has a purpose for me.

I was dealt another devastating blow while recovering from surgery. The doctor and hospital chaplain told me I have stomach cancer. I was shown results from my lab work and x-rays. I was told that due to the surgery there's a good chance it's spreading and if so it's terminal. The doctor spoke of treatment options, but couldn't say until we know if it's spreading. This still seems unreal to me. The chaplain sat with me and told me about Jesus. I told him how I Had prayed right after the attack. He put his hand on my arm and told me the Lord was with me. I felt God in his touch and I knew God had been there all along. Right then, with that chaplain, I fully and wholly asked the Lord to be in my heart. A lot of inmates have appeared to get, "jailhouse religion," but I assure you my faith and love for God is genuine. I got it the hard way. I came to prison in early 1998, at the age of 17 and fell into the prison ways. I got my faith and got saved because I needed saving.

I think Proverbs 16:18 says it best, "Pride goeth before destruction, and an haughty spirit before a fall." and Kim, what a fall I took! I had to go through alot to be humbled. I really thought I was something for a lot of years. I'm at

my lowest right now, but 1 Peter 5:6 makes a promise, "Humble yourselves therefore under the mighty hand of God, that He may exalt you in due time." I've almost accepted that I don't have much time left on this earth and I want to serve God until it's my time; with all my might. All I had was a much used bible, and a Kenneth Copeland magazine. So, I read 2 Corinthians 4:6, "*For God, who commanded the light to shine out of darkness, hath shined in our hearts, to give the light of the knowledge of the Glory of Go in the face of Jesus Christ.*" Then James 1:5,
"If any of you lack wisdom, let him ask of God; that giveth to all men liberally, and upbraideth not; and it shall be given him." That's all I needed! I began to pray for understanding and to be provided the tools necessary to learn and praise.

That's when another inmate sent me a copy of Free Life News. So, I prayed asking God if I should reach out to someone or does He want me to bear this alone. I felt in my heart I should reach out. So, I wrote the Free Life News people and I wrote a couple of churches that I read about in an O.K.C. newspaper. I know our God is faithful to us! Numbers 23:19, "*God is not a man, that He should lie; neither the sond of man, that He should repent Hath He said, and shall He not do it? or hath He spoken, and shall He not make it good?*" So, then Friday night I got a new copy of Free Life News the winder 2010 edition. I guess I'm on their mailing list now and praise God for your article spoke straight to me!

2 Corinthians 5:17 says, "Therefore If any man be in Christ, he is a new creation: old things are passed away; behold, all things are become new." I hope someone; just

one single person will rejoice when I die, knowing that I found God before I went. I guess that's the true message isn't it? I found salvation. God forgave me; of all people. God is no respecter of men; meaning what He will do for the preaching minister he will do for me also. That's powerful!

Hebrews 11:1, "Now faith is the substance of things hoped for, the evidence of things not seen." and what you said about faith not being something you do at church on Sunday, that it's every day and in all things. Proverbs 20:11, "Even a child is known by his doings, whether his works be pure, and whether it be right." As a Christian, we have to show, not confess, you confess something you have done wrong; you profess Jesus and show by His word and your life what is right and pure. Thank you for reading this. I take comfort in God's word in this trying time. The promise of John 3:16 and knowing that, "*the Lord is my Rock and my Fortress; and my Deliverer; My God, My Strength. In whom I will trust; my buckler and the horn of my Salvation, and my High Tower.*" Psalm 18:2 AMEN God Bless! Your Brother in Christ, Daryl Hess, OK

5 ERNESTO ALMAGUER

"Romans 6:4" From Death to Life

My name is Ernesto Almaguer, I am 32 yrs. Old and have found Jesus. I am really happy that He has given me this strength to share my testimony with you. Amen!! Before I came to Christ, I was a slave to sin. I was the devils puppet. He pulled my strings and controlled my life. He told me lies and used me. I've been in and out of prison all my life; even in my youth. I was 12 yrs. Old when I first got locked up. I was involved in gangs, sold drugs, and started doing drugs. I got hooked on heroin at the age of 18. I didn't care about my life or anyone else's. So, I continued my drug life and that got me deeper in the hole. I lost my family and committed crimes that led me to prison twice. At the time, I was still thinking I was a loser. I was filled with hate and anger and didn't care about the people I was hurting. But, I never knew it was the devil that was telling me those lies and blinding me from the love of Jesus.

Until, one day I heard someone speaking about Jesus in my cell, saying how much Jesus loves me no matter what I did in life. That if I would just let him in my heart and ask for forgiveness I would be a new person. I thought, "Yeah right. How can I become new? And why would Jesus love me after all the things I have done, and all the people I have hurt?" I tried to ignore Jesus, but something in my heart kept telling me to give in. I tried to fight it, but I started feeling funny and I started to tear up and out of nowhere I fell on my knees and cried like a baby. I told God I was sorry and if it's true I accept Jesus into my heart as my Lord and Savior. I felt His love upon me as I cried my heart out. That night I slept like a baby, and when I woke up everything felt better. I even felt 100 pounds lighter! It was a miracle and a blessing from God. I never knew how much love Jesus had for me. And now since I've given Him my life it's been amazing. He broke those chains that the devil had on me. He showed me that the devil tries to blind us so that we can't experience Jesus' love.

My life is now complete. I am no longer part of a gang, a junkie, or a slave to sin. Jesus paid for my sins and I am a child of God and He wants you to be His child too. Now, I trust Jesus to control my life; so I can do Gods will and tell someone else about this precious love. Don't you fall for satans lies all that fast money, the glamorous life isn't worth it. It all goes away. But, Jesus love is everlasting and I hope you will give Him a chance so that you can experience this wonderful love. May God bless you and know He is the only way through anything that you may be going through.

Your Brother in Christ! Ernesto Almaguer Jr.

The Power of God

First of all let us give thanks to our Almighty God for this wonderful blessing that He puts in our hearts, for this new day and for His strength, and most of all His precious love and mercy. Amen

I pray that as you read this testimony that whoever you are that the spirit of the Lord touches your heart. He is an awesome God! Amen! Right now He wants to come into your life and make you the person you should be through Him. He loves you with all His heart, so much that He sent His only son to die for you. (John 3:16) Can you imagine that? How amazing it is that our precious Father loves us and has mercy for us. Amen. No matter who you are, what you have done and even if you were saved and went astray; Jesus will always love you, forgive you and is waiting for you to let Him into your heart. (Rev. 3:20) Know this that the devil is a liar and doesn't want you to know Gods love. (John 8:44) all he wants to do is to destroy your life. (John 10:10) God has chosen you and wants to make you a new person. (jhn. 15:16, 2 Cor. 5:17) He wants you to be a part of His family and He has a plan for you (1Pet.2:9, Jer. 29:11) and He wants to do a new thing in you. (Isa.43:19)

Take it from this TDCJ third timer, former gang member, and drug addict: "Let GO! And Let GOD," lead you into your destiny. He laid down His life for you (jn 15:13) He bought you (1cor 6:20) with His blood (I pet 1:18-19) Why not give Him a chance so He can give you a new heart? (ezk 36:26) and a new mind (rom 12:1-2) and a new spirit (acts 1:5), new power (acts 1:8), new authority (Luke 10:19), and your hearts desires (ps 37:4). God wants a relationship with you (Jn 15:5-8), because He loves you. He will never leave you or forsake you. You've tried everything else, now try Jesus!!

I hope that you have been touched by Gods wonderful love. If you are willing to let Him in your life, and want to experience His love say this prayer, *"Dear God, I come before you as a sinner. I want a new life and I ask you to be in control of my life and show me Your way. Teach me your will and plan for my life so that I can be a witness to others. I accept your Son Jesus, and believe He died on the cross for my sins and arose on the third day, after defeating the powers of the devil in Hell. I accept you Jesus as my Lord and Savior and invite the Holy Spirit into my heart so that I may be made new and healed." Amen* If you said this prayer and believe you are saved, you are a child of God, Praise God! God Bless you. I love you all in Christ. Your Brother, Ernesto Almaguer Jr., La Mesa, Tx

6 FERNANDO BAUTISTA

I would like to tell you a little about me. I've been in and out of jail, this is my second time down, though I was out for 9 years; I was still living my own life, the way I wanted to. I used to go to church at Victory Outreach. God used them to bring me the Gospel, but I never knew God in a personal way. I went to church and tried to earn my righteousness by works; instead of by God's grace and mercies (Eph. 2:8-9). After I left the church I went on my own drug spree for many years and fell off (Matthew. 13:21-22). I really didn't understand scriptures; the way I do now. Due to Gods goodness, and faithfulness; He has opened up my eyes and now I know I've been set free to live a victorious new life. (Rom 6:1-11). The sin nature, or satan has no power over me unless I yield to them (Col. 2:14-15).

Jesus has made a way for those who hear His voice and follows Him, and I'm speaking truly follow Him. John 10:27-29). I understand the scriptures now and what its like to have a real relationship; only when serving Him out of love (1 Jhn.

2:3-6). I'm so greatful for the truth, because it has set me free (Jhn 8:32, 34-36). I know coming to prison wasn't my plans, but if God allowed this to happen, to work for the good (Rom. 8:28)…I give Him all the glory and praises. Though I really didn't know too much about my salvation, I just remember saying a simple sinner's prayer. I didn't truly know what I was or who I was without Jesus as my personal Savior. I know now that I'm a lost soul without Jesus. Many people are confused about what Salvation means. They think that because of Gods Grace they can continue to live in sin. Matthew 7:21-24 says otherwise; either you are in with all your heart, soul, and mind, or out.

7 JIMMY SMITH

I was born in Dallas, TX and I was raised in a small town called Duncanville. My parents did have a nice piece of land and we had chickens and a garden. But, I don't ever recall being considered ranchers or farmers. Mom always said we were just poor country folks. Growing up was pretty rough. My dad was never around much and when I did see him, he was drunk. He and my mother spent most of their time together cussing and screaming at each other. My father never could hold a job, because of his drinking and because he never learned to read and write; so this put most of the work on my mother.

My mother, at times would work two jobs, cook, clean and help me with my homework and see to it that I got to school. But, no matter how much my mom did to please my father; it never seemed to be enough. Never was church or God mentioned in our house as a kid. I love my father but he never failed to let me and my mother down. He constantly cussed and screamed at both of us. As a young boy, I wanted so bad to have my father's love that I clung to any male figure that would spend time with me.

My cousin and his wife lived just down the street and would occasionally come over to the house to visit. I remember them coming to the house and how my cousin would play ball with me and take me places. I also remember how he and his wife sexually abused me time after time. I remember how they threatened me, that if I told anyone that I would get into trouble. I also remember my cousin made fun of me after he would sexually assault me. The sexual abuse went on from the time I was six years old, until the time I was nine years old. Then they just stopped abusing me and coming over to visit. I guess they though that I would finally tell if they kept on abusing me. I was too scared of getting into trouble and too ashamed to ever tell anyone.

After the abuse stopped, I had so much anger and fear inside of me that I couldn't or wouldn't trust anyone. By the age of twelve, I was sniffing gasoline and glue and smoking marijuana. I became a kleptomaniac and a bully by the time I was 13 and I started using cocaine, acid, crystal and any other drug I could get my hands on. I tried to commit suicide at the age of fourteen, by taking 150 extra-strength Tylenol with codeine. But this just caused me more pain and several hours in the hospital with a tube up my nose and down my throat, to pump my stomach.

By the age of sixteen, I had been to jail at least a half a dozen times; for shoplifting. At eighteen years old, I received a ten year sentence for robbery and was on my way to Texas prison, because of my new habit of crack cocaine. At 22 years old, I was released from prison. Upon my release, I got a job, I got married and we had 2 beautiful children. But, I was still living a life of hurt, pain, anger and distrust. Eventually my marriage ended, my drug addictions increased and I became a total monster; not only in my own eyes but in everyone's eyes that knew me. I was literally trying to kill myself with drugs.

In the summer of 2000 that all changed and my life took a much needed dramatic turn. While sitting in a hotel room, waiting on my drug connection to bring me more drugs; I decided that I didn't want to live another day the way that I was living. So, I decided to blow my brains out with a Ruger 9mm. I remember looking in the mirror and hating the man that I had become. At that point I remember putting the gun in my mouth and putting my finger on the trigger. I began to cry and I asked God to help me end it. I squeezed that trigger with all the strength that I had, but the gun wouldn't fire.

God helped me end it as I had prayed. He didn't do it with a bullet. He did it in the form of His Son on the cross over 2000 years ago (John 3:16). With His great mercy and forgiveness. I carried the anger and hurt of being abused around with me for 30 years. Now at the age of 37, as I sit in a Texas prison with a life sentence for another robbery; I can honestly say that all the pain from a life of physical, mental, sexual and drug abuse is gone.

You see, God is a father to the fatherless. (Psalms 68:5) He is a light in a dark place. (Romans 2:19) He is the only one who can end your life the way it is now. He can end the hurt and the pain and replace it with His peace and joy. (John 14:27, Psalms 30:5)

Don't spend the rest of your life running from your past. If you don't have a past, you want have a future and if you don't have a future, then you will eventually return to your past. God says in His Word that He has plans and a future for us. (Jeremiah 29:11-14) He says that He came to set the prisoners free. (Psalms 146:7) That means you!

Today I am no longer a thief and a drug addict, but for the rest of my life I am a child of God. I thank God for the things He has done in me and I thank Him in advance for the things that He will do for you; if you will just ask for His help. I can finally breathe easy, think logically and have peace of mind.

8 KENNETH LEE

The Lord has been so merciful to me and has forgiven me much. Truly I love Him much! In 1989, I left temple, TX to see my daughter for what I believed to be the last time. On the freeway back to Dallas I closed my eyes hoping to crash and die. I became broken by my hopelessness. My eyes were further blinded by my tears. I cried unto the Lord, "God, I've got no place to go, no one to turn to. If you'll have me, I'll trust you." Surely His hands grabbed the steering wheel! His presence filled my heart. There came a great peace and calm in the midst of my storm! He embraced me in His arms of grace.

But, that was just the beginning. He freed me from lifelong bondages. He demolished the strongholds in my life that had me in prison. He took me out of the land of bondage and didn't take me out empty! He took me out full. He exploited the enemy. I went out, not by my own hand, but by the saving strength of His right Hand!

Like the parting of the Red Sea, I didn't have to go over through the mud and muck, I didn't have to crawl through. He lifted me up! He took me over onto dry land. He placed my feet on a solid rock. He took me clear over; that means all the way and clear through the Blood of Jesus! I will praise Him forever. Because my Redeemer lives I can face tomorrow. Because my Redeemer lives, all fear is gone. Though I'm in the midst of the Fire, I rejoice for He is with me.

Like the three children, I went in bound up; but I didn't fall down in the fire. For the King of Glory was present. Instead, I bow down to Him. The Fire of the enemy wanted to use and to destroy me, but the Lord used it to burn away my bonds. In His presence, I raise my hands in victory and I walk in the Fire having a talk with Jesus. Oh, in the fire I'm having a good time; in His presence! Though I will come out to proclaim His wonder, right now I'm enjoying His presence. If I was one of the children and was asked to come out, oh I'd be eager to as so just so I can tell the story. But, right now I'm in the presence of the Lord. I'll come out later! Where the Lord is I want to be. I told the Lord, "Lord, if you are fixing to show up on the Wynne Unit, if Your Glory is coming and you are about to bring a great Revival inside this prison, I don't want to miss it." I said these words when I was brought up for parole for the first time. For the past four years, I've been with a small group of Believers, praying for Revival on this unit and sweeping throughout the prisons of America. I truly want to be a part of every move of God. However, when I am released, I'm coming back into prisons to preach God's Word.

I've got the Scripture written on some boots, (Acts 5:19-20); these are my "Preaching Boots." They are reserved for God's use and I will preach until they fall off my feet as a witness unto the Lord! To Him be all the Glory.

God's Grace and Peace are yours. Stand firm, holding onto the hope we have in His coming. Your Brother in Christ, Kenn

9 MICHAEL TURNER

My childhood was a normal one, my mother and father loved me and the rest of my brother's and sister's. A family of seven, three boys and four girls, and my younger brother past away, physically, but not spiritually, he went on to be with the Lord, he died in his sleep. We will miss him, because he was a part of our family. I really didn't get a chance to get to know him, because he was taken so early, at the age of forty-four. We never know when the Lord will call us home, that's why He said to be ready, because you don't know if He's coming today or tomorrow, the Lord has given me peace about this whole ordeal. I haven't even shed a tear about my brother, I rejoice with confidence of an assurance knowing that our Heavenly Father has our loved ones with Him. This is the hope that's unseen and we should wait patiently for it; and while we wait for our Lord to appear, continue to bring forth Spiritual fruit.

My parents were just an ordinary couple to me. They were trying to raise a family of seven. Starting out was good. I never seen us have any hard times from what they let us kids know. My father had his own business, he had a moving business. We own our own store, we own our house, and our school was right in front of our house. So, it made it easy for our mother, she was a stay at-home mom. I think my grandmother stayed with us off and on. I really can't remember my father had a lot of antique cars, so we had a lot going on in our life. So, about this time my father wanted a relationship with God; there's nothing wrong with that, but my father wanted to follow Islam, a spiritual cult. So, our life now takes a turn we don't know anything about God. I don't even remember going to church as a child. We change schools, where the boys go to school in the morning and the girls went in the afternoon. That went on for a while. We didn't start having problems until me, my father and my two brothers went to see my uncle in prison; and when we returned home we learned that my mom and sisters took a trip themselves, and we waited patiently on their return. After they came back home that's when I remember everything started going bad. I don't know what my Father did, I think he did some underhanded stuff, because he went to jail for it. He didn't stay long and by then I was already in prison. He didn't even send me a letter; I seen him one time since I've been incarcerated. I've forgiven him, he's sick now and my only concern is if he has accepted our Lord and Savior Jesus Christ. I have wrote him and talked with him and he says he has; so I leave it alone.

They started selling everything, the cars, the truck, and the store. We moved out of town and stayed gone a few years and when we came back to Cleveland mom took the girls and dad took the boys. We stayed with our grandparents on his side; but you know when people start getting tired of you being around and I was starting to break into neighbors houses and then they said that I had to go and I don't remember where I went. I think I went to my grandmother's house where two of my little sisters stayed. My dad took me and my sisters with him out of town to look for my mom. We didn't find her, so we were headed back to Cleveland when the car broke down and my uncle from Indianapolis came and took us back to his house; my mother's sister. Everything was alright until my uncle found out that his wife was having an affair and he had a heart attack after unloading his gun into the man's car. My mom's sister lost her mind and we were sent to the detention center and we stayed there until my grandmother came and got us. My mom had a nervous break-down behind the affair my dad had and she hasn't really recover from it. The very one who birthed my mom is the one my father had the affair with; her mother. Now, I have been introduced to the real world and I grow up in juvenile detention home. I ran away from the group homes and I started stealing and sleeping in cars. I would sleep in people's basements, just to get out of the cold. I couldn't read or write. I haven't been in school since all these things took place in my life. I never stepped foot in my home room. My life is spinning out of control. I'm spending the night over at strangers houses; people I don't even know. They are the ones that introduce me to shooting dope, I was shooting up to $60 with a needle, they taught me how to cook, how to hit myself and once I learned that I didn't need them anymore. I learned where to buy it and then my habit was getting bigger and I wanted more.

Then, I bought a gun; that led me to robbing people and then I got my own apartment, using a prostitute. We got this apartment as a couple, and then I moved my two youngest sisters in with me. They didn't know I was shooting dope, but they found out. I would take them to school and would start robing all the way back home.

The things that I did; I'm not pleased with and the pain that my hand has caused those that were victims I deeply apologize for. My actions have cost me to miss out on being with my family and even a chance to have a family of my own. I don't have any kids, but the Lord's grace and mercy always see things through; the Lord is my best friend and I will never put my confidence in mankind. The Lord shows us who are real brothers and sister are, those who bear the fruit of the spirit.

10 SCOTT MESSER

When I was 8 years old, I went to live with my
grandparents. I don't know why; I just did. I lived with
my grandmother for 5 years. I had a good life, but I
didn't know why my mother sent me to live with my
grandmother. I now know that she does; but with the
mind of a child all I could come up with was that my
mother must not have loved me. I longed to live with
my mother, father and little brother and sister like other
normal families. So, when I was 13 years old I talked my
mother and my grandmother into letting me move back
in with my mother, step-father and my brother and
sister. I didn't know who my real Father was until I was
about 12 years old. Even after I found out who he was,
he still didn't want anything to do with me and still
doesn't. I have put him in our Heavenly Father's hands
now. I know that His perfect will is good whatever it is.
But, for years it really hurt me because he didn't love me
either.
When I turned 15, I met a girl. She was 14 and already
had 1 child and was expecting another. Although when I
met her I didn't know that she was pregnant. My
grandmother told me after I introduced them. I didn't

know how to look for that stuff at 15. We hadn't been intimate so I knew the baby wasn't mine. She told me that both children belonged to her father; that he'd been raping her. I didn't know what to do, but I knew that she needed help. The only thing I could think of at the time to help her was to marry her. We didn't think anybody would believe us if we told them what her dad was doing so we told everyone I was the babies daddy and we went to Donaldsonville, GA to get married; because in GA if the girl was with child you didn't need your parents' consent to get married back in 1982. So we got married I thought that I finally found someone who would appreciate me and love me after all I had given up for her. I had quit school, married her and went to work logging. Running a chain saw from daylight until dark. Seven days a week. For twenty-five dollars a day. That was the only job that a sixteen year old boy could get. As I was trying to support a wife and two children that weren't even mine. We didn't have a child until 1986. Then not long after our daughter was born everything started turning bad. I don't know why but my wife was sleeping around with my brother and cousin while I was at work. She said it would never happen again and I loved her and wanted to believe her, so I didn't divorce her and stayed with her; but I started drinking and using drugs heavily to cover up the pain. After that my life started spiraling out of control. She didn't stop sleeping around and I just wanted someone to love me; so I started having affairs as well and telling my-self with each woman that this one will love me. If I would have known then that my Heavenly Father already loved me unconditionally, my life might have been a lot different. By the time I was 24, I was already an angry and bitter man. I had made the decision that nobody loved me and never would; no matter what I did. So, I stopped caring. I figured, if no one was ever going to love me, why should I care about anyone else. Of course my grandmother and my mother and my daughter did care about me; but I wasn't thinking about that. I couldn't see through the anger, hatred and bitterness; that was inside of me. If only I would have cried out to God, I would have known; but I couldn't love a God, or believe that He loved me. Who would allow me to go through life thinking no one would ever love me.

So, in 1990 I went to prison on multiple charges for 5 ½ years. That just made me more angry and bitter. I did everything in prison that I did in the world and even worse. I continued my drug and alcohol abuse in prison and when I got out I was even worse than before. I literally hated pretty much every one and all I wanted to do was to hurt people, like I had been hurt. I felt that everyone should pay for what I had went through. Now, as I look back, I think what my Lord and Savior Christ Jesus went through for the sins of the whole world; including mine. The love I longed for was right before my eyes but I couldn't see it through the pain and anger, and bitterness that was in my heart.

My wife got pregnant by another man while I was in prison and divorced me. When I got out in December 1992 I was angrier than ever. I moved in and lived in a sinful relationship with another woman. In August 1993 eight months after I got out of prison, my ex-wife called me from Tallahassee, FL and told me that her boyfriend had left her stranded there with nowhere to go. I remarried her and before long she was sleeping with my brother, uncle and all my friends again. So, I dealt with it by getting drunker and using drugs. I went on a 5 week binge after she left me for another man again and I woke up in jail. I got another prison sentence of fifteen years this time. My wife divorced me again. This time I read my bible a little bit, but I still felt like nobody loved me. I got out of prison in 2004, after serving 9 ½ years this sentence. I did good for the first year I didn't drink or use any drugs. I found a good job, made good money and bought a new truck, got a couple of credit cards, had a checking and savings account, and a nice apartment. Then I got a new girlfriend and the cycle started all over again. She was married she said to an abusive husband so I chose to let her live with me in an adulterous relationship. I later found out that she was addicted to pain medicine after she ran off with all my money and she used up my credit cards. Back came the fear, anger, pain, hurt and bitterness. Because I wasn't relying on Jesus Christ, my heart wasn't protected and I went back to drugs and alcohol. Within thirty days I was back in jail. This time I was facing a life sentence. I gave up on life, I just didn't care anymore.

Until the chaplain came to ad seg. and got me moved to the faith based dorm. I participated in the program and read my bible, because I felt obligated to the chaplain to do so. I prayed to God about my sentence, I didn't want to spend the rest of my life in prison. I said God alright if you are real and it is your will, provide me a way to get the attorney I need so I want have to spend the rest of my life in prison. A couple of days later I called home and my grandmother told me, "Son we got you that lawyer." She had sold her house to get me an attorney; so I wouldn't have to spend the rest of my life in prison. While I spent all those years believing that nobody cared or loved me. On November 4, 2009 I was sentenced to ten years prison! The following January 2010, I asked Jesus Christ into my heart and life as my personal Lord and Savior. My grandmother, mother and daughter come to see me when they can and now I am at peace. I've given all my problems and burdens to the Lord. God really has blessed me.

Jeremiah 29:11-13 says, "For I know the plans I have for you, plans to prosper you and not to harm you, plans to give you hope and a future. Then you will call upon me and come and pray to me, and I will listen to you. You will seek me and find me, when you seek me with all your heart."

LESSONS FROM THE BIBLE

FAITH

HOPE

LOVE

11. Intro to

Faith, Hope and Love.....

.....these three words definitely define the foundation for Christian living. They should be our stronghold, as Jesus Christ. So many times; like today, I feel that I've failed in most of these areas. It's easy to tell someone else how they should act or behave. But, how do I react and behave when faced with my own personal challenges and struggles? Do I act the way I tell others to; the way that I know I should or do I give in to the weaknesses of my flesh? Today I acted ungodly, unloving and do not feel strong in faith or hope. Who am I to teach others, when I am such a failure; in so many ways and areas? I am nobody God! I came from dirt and will return to the same. This world isn't my home! I just don't know sometimes why my flesh takes over and my spirit man seems so distant, so weak. I know these things that I say or do are wrong but yet it's like I can't stop my mouth from speaking or my body from reacting in a way that is not loving or kind. What kind of witness does that make me? What kind of wife or mother? I am a failure. I am nothing without Christ Jesus. I am sorry Father, for my trespasses are so many and I need your help to overcome this flesh of pride and evilness. Please help me be more like you Jesus, loving and kind and humble and selfless. I want to be described in this way; if only I could surrender all to you. Just like the song, "I surrender all," but for real, not just in singing but in spirit and body and mind and flesh. Why must I be so weak? Always saying and doing the wrong things! We always have a choice to love or to offend. I cannot say that I commonly choose to love over my misfortune to offend. Am I a failure amongst saints? Maybe.....but I believe that I am not alone in this area of battle. I long so much to be good and like the bible says we can be and should be! But, it's by grace that we are even aloud to be children of the Most High God. So even in my suffering and personal torment God is good and loving and faithful and so I must lean on Him and rely on Him for my lack of sufficiency. I do not know how to be, except by His love I am set free; from the chains of slavery. I am free to rejoice in Him through my pain and my failures and look at His Holy Word and invite His presence; to make me whole and even dare I say Holy. Faith, Hope and Love these are the foundation of a Christian believer's walk with God; the Father, Son and Holy Spirit. Jesus Christ is the way, the truth and the life, no one can get to the Father except through Him! John 14:6 I hope that this personal message of real struggle will help somebody today. Kim B. Fincher

"*10*In conclusion, be strong in the Lord [be empowered through your union with Him]; draw your strength from Him [that strength which His boundless might provides].   *11*Put on God's whole armor [the armor of a heavy-armed soldier which God supplies], that you may be able successfully to stand up against [all] the strategies and the deceits of the devil.   *12*For we are not wrestling with flesh and blood [contending only with physical opponents], but against the despotisms, against the powers, against [the master spirits who are] the world rulers of this present darkness, against the spirit forces of wickedness in the heavenly (supernatural) sphere.   *13*Therefore put on God's complete armor, that you may be able to resist and stand your ground on the evil day [of danger], and, having done all [the crisis demands], to stand [firmly in your place].   *14*Stand therefore [hold your ground], having tightened the belt of truth around your loins and having put on the breastplate of integrity and of moral rectitude and right standing with God,   *15*And having shod your feet in preparation [to face the enemy with the firm-footed stability, the promptness, and the readiness produced by the good news] of the Gospel of peace.   *16*Lift up over all the [covering] shield of saving faith, upon which you can quench all the flaming missiles of the wicked [one].   *17*And take the helmet of salvation and the sword that the Spirit wields, which is the Word of God.   *18*Pray at all times (on every occasion, in every season) in the Spirit, with all [manner of] prayer and entreaty. To that end keep alert and watch with strong purpose and perseverance, interceding in behalf of all the saints (God's consecrated people).   *19*And [pray] also for me, that [freedom of] utterance may be given me, that I may open my mouth to proclaim boldly the mystery of the good news (the Gospel),   *20*For which I am an ambassador in a coupling chain [in prison. Pray] that I may declare it boldly and courageously, as I ought to do." Ephesians 6:10-20 (Amplified)

12.

LESSONS

ON

FAITH

Forgiveness

We are taught in our society, to be strong and do it ourselves. I've come to realize; after spending almost 3 years in prison that I need help. Today I depend on God for my strength and Jesus Christ for my hope.

"13Therefore put on God's complete armor, that you may be able to resist and stand your ground on the evil day [of danger], and, having done all [the crisis demands], to stand [firmly in your place]." Ephesians 6:13

I am living free by God's guidance. I find it in His word, in spirit-filled believers and time spent alone with God in prayer and contemplation. My heart has been broken and abused by myself and by many people in my life. Now that I can no longer rely on alcohol, drugs, and bad relationships to handle my pain and hurt; I must fully rely on God.

How do we heal the pain in our heart? Take a minute to contemplate this question and write a few sentences down. Now, let's read Luke 7:3-4 in order to understand how to forgive as is written in God's holy bible. It is important that we have faith to forgive, accept, imagine, (believe the) truth, and (ask for God's) help.

This first lesson we will cover forgiveness and we will study Titus to illustrate how to forgive and live more Godly lives. Let's take a minute to read Titus 1 now. In this letter Paul is writing to Titus, after his first release form a Roman prison (Acts 27). He starts out with a powerful greeting, "in the hope of eternal life that God, who never lies, promised before the ages began." Titus 1:2 Then Paul reviews Titus' work in Crete, where he explains the qualifications for elders, Titus 1:5-9 and exposes false teachers Titus 1:10-16.

Now, let's read Titus 2. In this chapter Paul instructs Titus on teaching various groups. Verses 11-14 are worth rereading and writing down for further contemplation on. " *11For the grace of God (His unmerited favor and blessing) has come forward (appeared) for the deliverance from sin and the eternal salvation for all mankind.*

12It has trained us to reject and renounce all ungodliness (irreligion) and worldly (passionate) desires, to live discreet (temperate, self-controlled), upright, devout (spiritually whole) lives in this present world,

13Awaiting and looking for the [fulfillment, the realization of our] blessed hope, even the glorious appearing of our great God and Savior Christ Jesus (the Messiah, the Anointed One)."

Okay, let's stop right here and address forgiveness. Do you think that Paul had to be forgiving as a servant of God? If you will recall from the intro and after reading acts 27, Paul was in prison not too long before writing this letter to Titus. What will it take for you to forgive yourself, others and to be forgiven?

Acceptance

" *¹¹For the grace of God (His unmerited favor and blessing) has come forward (appeared) for the deliverance from sin and the eternal salvation for all mankind.*

¹²It has trained us to reject and renounce all ungodliness (irreligion) and worldly (passionate) desires, to live discreet (temperate, self-controlled), upright, devout (spiritually whole) lives in this present world,

¹³Awaiting and looking for the [fulfillment, the realization of our] blessed hope, even the glorious appearing of our great God and Savior Christ Jesus (the Messiah, the Anointed One)
Titus 2:11-13

Take a moment to get down on your knees and ask God for guidance and thank the Lord for his love and protection. Pray for the ability to accept the things that you cannot change, the courage to change the things you can and the wisdom to know the difference. Remember as we discussed in the last lesson on Forgiveness that we must let go of resentment and anger and let God heal our hearts. Our Father God wants us to experience joy and feel blessed as He blesses us each day; with so much to be thankful for. We just have to take the time to breath it all in. Take a moment and do that right now and make a list of all the things that you need to accept right where you are at.

Let's turn to a bible verse on Kingdom Standards or Kingdom living. Now this "Kingdom" is referring to God's Holy kingdom and us as his children.

1 Corinthian 6:9-11

"⁹Do you not know that the unrighteous and the wrongdoers will not inherit or have any share in the kingdom of God? Do not be deceived (misled): neither the impure and immoral, nor idolaters, nor adulterers, nor those who participate in homosexuality,

¹⁰Nor cheats (swindlers and thieves), nor greedy graspers, nor drunkards, nor foulmouthed revilers and slanderers, nor extortioners and robbers will inherit or have any share in the kingdom of God.

¹¹And such some of you were [once]. But you were washed clean (purified by a complete atonement for sin and made free from the guilt of sin), and you were consecrated (set apart, hallowed), and you were justified [pronounced righteous, by trusting] in the name of the Lord Jesus Christ and in the [Holy] Spirit of our God."

1 Corinthian 6:17, 19-20

"¹⁷But the person who is united to the Lord becomes one spirit with Him. ¹⁹Do you not know that your body is the temple (the very sanctuary) of the Holy Spirit Who lives within you, Whom you have received [as a Gift] from God? You are not your own,

²⁰You were bought with a price [purchased with preciousness and paid for, made His own]. So then, honor God and bring glory to Him in your body."

Imagine

"I can only imagine what my life would be..." is a popular Christian song by Mercy Me. It touches base on our topic on Imagine. "*I can do all things through Christ Jesus who strengthens me.*" Phil. 4:13. Take a moment and imagine your life without a savior and maybe take some notes of actually how it was before you were saved. My list would begin September 27th, 1979 to September 23, 2007, when Jesus took me out of the pits of Hell and brought me to The Father God.

Now take a moment to review the beginning scriptures from the lesson on acceptance: Titus 2:11-13. God's image of man took 7 days to realize, read with me from the beginning: *Genesis 1:1*, "*In the beginning God created the heavens and the earth.*" vs. 27 "*So God created man in his own image, in the image of God he created him; male and female he created them.*" *Gen. 2:2*, "*By the seventh day God had finished the work he had been doing; so on the seventh day he rested from all his work.*"

I encourage you to read on through Genesis, you will read about Adam and Eve in Chpt. 2. The Fall of Man in Ch. 3, Cain and Abel in Ch. 4, From Adam to Noah in Ch. 5. Let's stop at Ch. 6 and read a very important spin in history, The Flood vs. 5-8. And we'll end our study at Genesis 10.

Now, imagine for a moment what our lives would be like today if Noah wouldn't have found favor with God. He was the one man on earth who walked with God. Wow! That truly amazes me!! Does it you?

Now imagine your life outside those prison walls and write down your vision, your goals, and your dreams. Take what you have written down and give them to God in prayer. Ask for His guidance and will be done in your life. Ask for strong faith and discernment and for all people and doors that are not of Him to be removed from your life and the doors and people that are of Him to be made known. God's will and plan is the best there is. Believe that He will keep you safe and He will answer your prayers in His Divine timing; if it is His will, which is always for our best.

To help you do that, pick a Psalms to meditate on every day for the next month; from Psalms 121-Psalms 131. Write it down and you might want to choose different psalms each week. Sing it, read it, pray it, and believe it. God's words are alive and real! Believe them and know them as real, in your heart and spirit and no matter what trials and hardships you experience on the inside, you will not be separated from your Father God's love and His truth. Keep it close to your heart; wear it as your armor of protection. Eph. 6 and you will make it through this time and so much more!

Further Readings: John 3:16-21 Read and meditate on this and then Revelations 22:12-21.

Do not despair, imagine Jesus night and day and live by His ways. There isn't an easy road to eternal life, but theirs much peace and truth found in the Holy Word of God. Open the Holy bible today and seek Gods will and truth for your life.

Truth

As I sit, in a much better condition today than before I knew Jesus Christ as my Savior; I think of you, (those who are in prison and struggling with their faith). Yesterday morning's sermon at Church inspired me to write my purpose as God's servant. Jesus came to me in my greatest despair. He interceded on my behalf with God.

His love for me gave me strength, to have faith and let the Holy Spirit heal my heart.

His mercy gave me the courage to face another day in prison. He filled me with hope that I could survive that hell; another day, another week, another month and another year.

His Holy Bible spoke words of wisdom and truth that brought light to my eyes and gave me a purpose and a path to follow.

The truth is I chose to serve God while in prison. I was in prison by my past choices. Once, I was able to see God's truth from the Holy Bible; I chose to serve Him and His truth became my truth. I prayed for God to use me, each day and I still do. I prayed for God to forgive my sins and I repented of the wrongs I've done and began to make amends to each person I'd done wrong.

The people I couldn't write to, I prayed about and spoke to God about in prayer; as if I was speaking to Him directly. As I played my life's truth out, the memories came, over and over again in my head. I began to see things differently, over time. When I slept I invited the Holy Spirit to rest within me and to fill me with visions of God's Will, so that I could be of use.

I devoted hours and days to silently meditating on scriptures and books in the Bible. I got to know the prophets and servants in the Old Testament that God had chosen and who believed and followed God's Laws. I celebrated Jesus' birth on Christmas; by reading the four Gospels: Mathew, Mark, Luke and John and writing down scripture verses from them on little pieces of paper and sharing them with my neighbors.

I got so excited with the forthcoming of Jesus' return that I dreamed about it and woke up some mornings asking God and hoping that this would be the day. He would tell me, "Not until all have heard about my son." The enemy satan would attack me on many occasions, as I struggled to find my way through the deception and lies around me; as a new believer. I rested at the feet of my Savior; under His wings of shelter, allowing time for old and new wounds to heal. So that my past wasn't my future or what defined me. I learned to live in the presence of my Creator.

I pray that during this time in your life you will seek God first and let him show you the way and that you will know your truth and see His truth as your own. Truth meaning what defines your lifestyle, your values and beliefs; that are your truth: what you understand to be true and real. Make use of the resources available to you and the unique fellowship opportunities. Freedom is made real through God's grace. Once you believe in life through the world, you will seek worldly possessions.

53

If you know God's truth and believe in freedom through the blood salvation of Jesus Christ and know that eternal life is more valuable than stored up worldly goods, then you will be free no matter where you are. In this state of belief, freedom lives within your heart and is defined by your faith and trust in God.

You will focus on His plan and Will for your life and not put so much value and importance on what the world says defines freedom.

Scriptures to Study: Joshua 1:1-9, I Peter 1:1-9, II Corinthians: 4:1-9, Revelation 19:1-9. 20:1-9, 21:1-8

Healing

Sometimes the only way for us to heal is for something dramatic to happen to us. An event that will have us running to God and begging him day and night for a miracle. Sometimes healing takes a miracle. We will read some scriptures about these types of healing miracles:

Acts 4:14 *"But since they could see the man who had been healed standing there with them, there was nothing they could say."*

Read all of Acts 3; Acts 3:6, *"Then Peter said, "Silver or gold I do not have, but what I have I will give you. In the name of Jesus Christ of Nazareth, walk." Acts 3:16 "By faith in the name of Jesus, this man whom you see and know was made strong. It is Jesus' name and the faith that comes through him that has given this complete healing to him, as you can all see."* Continue on reading Acts 4; Acts 4:20 *"For we cannot help speaking about what we have seen and heard."* 4:22 *"For the man who was miraculously healed was over 40 years old."* Vs.30 *"Stretch out your hand to heal and perform miraculous signs and wonders through the name of your holy servant Jesus."*

From these 2 chapters in the Book of Acts it is clear to see that Peter and Paul believed in miraculous signs and healings through speaking of their faith in Jesus Christ. What do you believe?

Let's go to another story in the old testament. This story exemplifies the power of one man's faith in God Almighty. <u>Begin reading at 1 Samuel 17:4 through vs 51.</u> And then focus on these verses 45-47 and then vs. 50. Now can you tell me, did David have faith that caused a miracle to happen? Oh Yes he did! Why do you think this was? Go back to vs. 34-37 for the answer. God had rescued him before and He knew that God would be with him now. In both of these historical stories we read about men of God who have faith and their faith bringing miracles. Do you have the faith it takes to receive a miracle? If no, why not?

I would like you to pick out 5-10 scriptures on faith and healing to write down, circle, read out loud and meditate on for a month and the more that you know these scriptures and believe them for your life, the more that you can expect and receive a miracle in the name of Jesus! Let me give you some suggestions of scriptures that help me believe in God's power through the blood of Jesus to heal.

- Psalms 91:9-12 let me know I am safe and protected from harm by God
- Ephesians 1:19-21 God's power is greater than the powers of this world
- John 3:16-21 Reminds me that there's an eternal reward for the good I do
- Philippians 4:6-9 Puts my priorities straight when I get off track
- Revelation 7:13-17 Gives me hope in what is to come

Now these scriptures give me a strong foundation of beliefs and values to set the stage for me to receive healing. I encourage you to stay prayed up and "scriptured- up," so that when the enemy comes knocking on your door, you will have the antidote waiting for his venomous attack and no harm will be done to you; in the name of Jesus! This takes dedicated focus on the word of God. I know that you have what it takes, because you are a child of the Most High God. Now for healing stories turn to the good old gospels, they are filled with Jesus' miracles and healings. It's a good place to start and then you might like to venture into the old testament, in books like Judges and Kings or other books in the new testament. Go where the Lord leads you and have fun while you explore God's words and truths for healing.

Jesus is Alive In God's temple that's You & Me! We pray for you that this ministry is of encouragement in your time of need.

SUMMARY

Jesus came to me in my greatest despair. He interceded on my behalf with God. His love for me brought me strength, to have faith and let the Holy Spirit heal my heart. His mercy gave me the courage to face another day in prison. He filled me with hope that I could survive this hell; another day, another week, another month, and even another year. His Holy Bible spoke words of wisdom and truth to my mind that brought light to my eyes and gave me a purpose and a path to follow as His servant.

The truth is God saved me from myself and satan. He showed me His truth and satans lies, that I was believing and dying from living by. His Holy Bible became my sword and weapon against satans lies. I chose to serve Him and His truth became my truth. I prayed for God to use me each day and I still do. I prayed for God to forgive my sins and I repented of the wrong's I've done and began to make amends to each person I could. The people I couldn't contact by writing I prayed for their forgiveness as if I was talking to them in person; but God heard me and the weight's lifted from my heart and the heavy burden of guilt I'd been carrying. When I slept at night I invited the Holy Spirit to rest in God's temple (me) and that I would receive visions of God's will for my life. I got to know my ancestors, the prophets and saints from the old and new testaments. I celebrated Jesus' birth on Christmas, by reading all of the four Gospels and writing down scriptures from them and sharing them with other inmates.

I hope that you are seeing the picture that I am drawing for you, of my life after Christ; right there in prison. I got so excited about salvation and the coming of Jesus I would eagerly pray for it to be today to God. God would whisper in my ear, "not yet there are more who need to hear the Good News about Jesus." So, I would gather neighbors and have bible studies and pray for people to know Jesus. My truth was God and His work right where I was. There wasn't anything better for me to do. The enemy satan would attack me on many occasions through lies and deceptions. But, I rested at my Father's feet and stayed in the word; as I do now. My past was no longer what defined me. I had the blood of Jesus protecting me and covering me. I learned to live more in the presence of my Creator. I pray that right now you will begin to seek God and put Him first! That you will let Him show you the way to truth and freedom. The Holy bible contains all of God's truth that is there for you to reap from its wisdom and obtain its hope for you. If you will focus on His plan for you, life will be much more valuable and you will experience joy like never before. His love will set you free and fill you up. Give Jesus a try!

Truth is what you see and believe. God's word contains innumerable truths that can be utilized and beneficial to your daily circumstances and situation; wherever you are. The freedom that begins with Jesus Christ as your personal savior ends in eternity. We are given a chance on earth to seek God and know Jesus so that we will spend the rest of our existence in Heaven.

13.

LESSONS

ON

HOPE

Asking God for Help

1 Sam. 8:7-9 "and the Lord told Samuel, "Listen to whatever the people say to you. They have not rejected you. They have rejected me from being their king. They are doing as they have always done. When I took them out of Egypt, they left me and served other gods. They are doing the same to you." continue reading chapter 8.

God gives us what we want and when we reject Him we are relying on people for help and people will always disappoint and never give us the love of God who is always there. Samuel talked to God directly that's how close He was to God. The people of Israel asked Samuel for what they wanted instead of accepting that God was already their king; they wanted to be like the other nations and have a physical king.
Samuel warned the people of what the king who ruled over them would do against them. vs. 10-18. "But the people would not listen to Samuel. They said, "No! We want a king to rule over us. Then we will be the same as all the other nations. Our king will judge for us and go with us and fight our battles."

Doesn't this sound like what we are doing today too? We want to be like the people on tv or our neighbors. Are we eager to please our family and friends but struggle when it comes to having faith and turning to God for help? I know I was and still am sometimes. We think that we can do it ourselves, we don't need anybody's help. If we only realized what God has waiting for us: the blessings, the healing, the love, the miracles if we could see all this we'd be running to Him but that requires faith as small as a mustard seed.

Continue reading 1 Sam. 12-15 and you will read how the people's king was rejected by God and just how life was for Israel without accepting God as their King. I love chapter 12, Samuel's Farewell Speech. He served God and as a servant of God He was the intercessor for the people to God and from God to the people. Well Israel wanted a king and so that's what God gave them a man to rule and lead over them. verses 16-20 and really gives a vision of Samuels relationship with God and how fearful the people were of him and his God. In chapter 14 is another example of a man's strong faith in God and how God blesses those who believe in Him and obey His ways. vs. 6 and 12 are Jonathan affirming with confidence His faith in God to help them and deliver them from their enemies. vs. 15 and 20 show God's faithfulness in delivering Jonathan and his men and vs. 23 sums it up. "So the Lord saved the Israelites that day..." Notice how Saul was busy with his comforts of the flesh (vs. 2) and didn't even know his son Nathan had left the camp and how he was quick to join in on the action (vs. 20) but it was Jonathan's faith in action that saved them that day. (vs.6, 12-14)

Now lets go to the new testament and read about the importance of Jesus Christ in our lives today when we are turning to God for help. Col. 1:11 "God will strengthen you with his own great power so that you will not give up when troubles come, but you will be patient." Sometimes we just need to be patient and be still to allow God's divine timing to work in our lives. Now let's read verses 15-20. It says that through Jesus Christ we are brought back to God. It's so important for us to know that when we pray to God we must do it through Jesus Christ. Otherwise, were just praying to any spirit that claims to be a god and that's not the one true God, thats satan and if in our hearts we don't yet know Jesus as our savior we are an open door for satans attacks. We need to be specific with our creator and father God so their's no mistake who we believe in and who we are serving each day.

Now if we turn to Romans 6-8 we get a more in depth reading of who we are as christ-like people. Rom. 6:verse 16 speaks about being a slave to sin verses following God and having freedom. Rom. 7:15-18 talks about the struggle we have with sin in our bodies (flesh) and the importance of knowing and standing on our faith in God through Jesus Christ vs. 25. Chapter 8: We have a choice to be ruled by sin or to serve God. vs. 37-39 says nothing can seperate us from the love of God through Christ Jesus our Lord.

So, take hope in our salvation through Jesus and from stories about peoples strong faith from the old testament. Read Job if you haven't or reread it if you have and be amazed at someone's faith in God and how God blesses and loves our faith. Satan can't kill us if we are true to God, he only has the power we give him through our lack of hope in God.

Do not give the devil any power in your life stand up and shout unto God right where you are today make a scene if that's what it takes for you to believe in God for help. People can laugh but they will be crying soon after wanting what we have the love of God and salvation through Jesus. Never forget the greatest help of all comes from the one who created us and lives within us and knows our hearts. Praise God today and he will surely bless you!!

Obeying God

Isaiah 42:7 *"You will help the blind to see. You will free those who are in prison, and you will lead those who live in darkness out of their prison."*

This scripture is a witness to JKF Prison Ministry. While I was in prison our Father God gave me a vision of this ministry. He spoke to me about the newsletter I've been writing now since June 2009- *Words of Encouragement.* I was obedient to his message and guidance to me. Before leaving prison I collected the names of about 20 girls from the unit I was on and I wrote them each and sent them the newsletter. Then later God used me to create these bible study series on Faith, Hope and Love.
Now were talking about: <u>Obeying God</u>.
There are steps that we must take, as we build a relationship with God, through Jesus Christ the Son of God and man.
<u>First:</u> Salvation & Repentance, Sinner's Prayer-Accepting Jesus Christ as your Savior (the Holy Spirit takes residence in us-God's creation and temple) *(John 3:3)*

<u>Second:</u> Baptism with water *(John 3:16)*

<u>Third:</u> being filled with the Holy Spirit (baptism with fire-an overflowing) & Receiving the gifts of the Spirit: speaking in tongues, visions, prophecy, discernment, healing

<u>Fourth:</u> Reading God's Holy Bible daily and asking for God's wisdom as you read to know what the scriptures are saying for your life personally

<u>Fifth:</u> Praying for God's will for your life and guidance daily

<u>Sixth:</u> Listening for God's answers and being obedient to His will

<u>Seventh:</u> Using your spiritual gifts: speaking in tongues, receiving visions, encouraging others, teaching. Allowing God to use you to (witness) helping others as you continue to grow, heal and shine with God's Spirit of truth and your salvation through Jesus Christ.

Now these steps aren't the exact perfect order, but they are all necessary for you to build a full-relationship with God through Jesus. You might even have an understanding of these steps, but more importantly God wants you to have a personal experience with visions as you obey our Father God and hear His voice speaking His will for your life to you directly into your heart and spirit! Nothing compares to this!!

Please read: all of *Acts 10* now focus on *vs. 3-4* about Cornelius and *vs. 22*. Now read *vs. 27-28* again about Peter's vision from God and *vs. 33-35* on both of their obedience to God's visions to them.

Acts 10:44-48 As Peter was speaking to the non-jewish people the Holy Spirit came down on all of them and they began to speak in tongues praising God. They were then baptized with water in the name of Jesus Christ. I would now like you to turn to *John 14* so we can get some words from Jesus Christ Himself about our Father God and the Holy Spirit.

Read: John 14: *1, 6, 12*

Vs.6 This is why we must always pray Dear Father God in the name of Jesus. We do not pray directly to Jesus we pray to the Father through Jesus.

Vs.12 Jesus was saying that we have power to do exactly what He did while on earth: casting out demons, healing people, power over temptations of the body and of the devil by our faith in Him and asking our Father in His (Jesus') name.

Read: *John 14:15-17, 26* talks about the Holy Spirit, the Spirit of truth only known to those who believe in Jesus and pray to the Father God in the name of Jesus.

Patient Endurance

Jesus endured so much in the world. Imagine knowing your purpose is to die a painful and cruel death. Jesus did and when the time came near he went to pray alone on the Mount of Olives with His disciples close by. He told them to pray for strength against temptation, as He went and prayed to the Father God this prayer: "Father, if you are willing, take away this cup of suffering. But do what you want, not what I want." *Luke 22:42* What patient endurance He had! If we only had an ounce of His great patience to endure through the troubled times and hardships; we'd be on cloud nine. It reminds me of all the prophets who denied their calling to serve God and how God had patient mercy on them and used them anyway. Lets look at a couple for inspiration and encouragement.

Read Jonah: a prophet to the ten northern tribes of Israel, he ran from God and ended up in a whales belly for 3 days, then obeyed God and was upset of His mercy on the people who feared God. Read Exodus 2-4 Moses: a prophet to the Jews (Israel), he murdered an egyptian and fleed, when God called Him he questioned God's call to use him. Moses begged God that he wasn't a good speaker and said "Please, Lord, send someone else." *Exodus 4:13* the Lord used him to free the Israelites from the Egyptian King and delivered the 10 Commandments to them. *Read Exodus 20: 1 21*

When God's words come to me they're not planned by my will; they're of God's will and timing. I just write them in obedience as His servant. This requires patient endurance. Today my flesh wanted so much to be in control instead of listening to God's wisdom. I wanted to do something now, so I thought of all these different people I could call and talk to and the Lord spoke to me as I was reading *Jeremiah 36:6*, "on the day of fasting;" to turn my phone off and focus on Him. So I immediately obeyed Him turning off my phone and praying for His will. It's not always easy to follow God's guidance and will; but once you begin doing it you'll know that it's the right thing to do always. It's hard for me staying home as a full-time Mom; but I'm doing it by faith in God as He guided me to do so and I know it's the best thing for me and my family.

Patience isn't my best quality so I ask for God's help. Taking a deep breath I ask the Lord for guidance to patiently endure. Sometimes my mind starts wondering to wanting a job or to be single and go back to school full-time as a student; but that's the past. I prayed for a husband and a family and God has blessed me with both. Now, I've got to keep my eyes on the Lord and move forward attending to the Kingdom business. Sometimes that means changing 3 dirty diapers in an hour as a mom or cooking a meal and cleaning the house as a wife and praying over a sister or brother in Christ as a servant of God but above all I am a Servant of God as a wife, mom and sister in Christ.
Just remember this: "I can do all things through Christ, because he gives me strength." *Phil. 4:13* and "Seek first God's kingdom and what God wants. Then all your other needs will be met as well." *Matth. 6:33*

14.

LESSONS

ON

LOVE

Letting go and letting God

When you give your heart to God and accept Jesus Christ as your savior you have to let go of all the resentment and frustrations from your life and when you go back to your job and home you're a new person in Christ. The old you has died and the people around you sometimes will look at you crazy and think you've lost your mind and as the word says, "we are fools for Christ's sake." 1 Cor. 4:10

Read: John 14 The answered prayer. Please reflect on Jesus' message

Joseph says "I gave my resentments away to Jesus and along with that all the resentments from work I had to completely surrender all sins. I then had to learn everything all over again; even tasks I knew before from work. They didn't understand that I'd lost memories to do with work as I gave it all to God. A lot of my resentments and sins had to do with my job and when I surrendered my life and gave those resentments away some of my work knowledge went with my resentments and sins because they were attached. Really I was learning life all over again and I still am."

Having to learn everything over again; how to live, is a real part of letting go and letting God feel you with His living water of love and the holy spirit. We've got to stay close to the Father in prayer, not to allow the enemy in to destroy God's grace in our lives. We are also called to be humble like it says in John 13:14-17. We are to be servants. We've got to let go of our pride and our will to serve God's greater plans and will. Every day we are to get closer to Jesus as we learn to love like He did on earth. Everyone isn't going to accept who we are in Christ but that's ok. We've got to press on focusing on the narrow path to eternal life and the glorious light in Christ Jesus. Praise God!!

Letting go of sin is a real struggle. Satan is around the corner waiting to take you back in the darkness and he will use those moments when you are tired and vulnerable to beat you over the head with memories of old sins that you enjoyed and maybe you just haven't completely given God a certain part of your life. Now is the time.

Here are some scriptures that might help you as they have helped me with addressing and letting go of sin in my life.

Psalm 101:2-4, Psalm 102:19-20, 28, Psalms 103:3, 10, 12, 17-18, Revelation 20:3, James 3:10, 13, James 4:7-8 and all of Malachi and Jeremiah 27.

We bring you the love of Christ Jesus!

Other people's opinions

Do you constantly worry about what <u>they</u> will think or what <u>they</u> will say? Have you ever watched the British comedy called, Keeping up Appearances? It is an extreme example of an old lady who is always worried about her neighbor's opinions and they just think she's crazy and really she is. Worrying about what other people think is a good way to go crazy! We shouldn't have time to worry so much about other people's opinions. When we focus on what's really important and matters as it is written in the good book of wisdom and truth; that would be the Holy Bible we will learn from Solomon in Ecclesiastes how to balance out our life chapter 3 tells us theirs a time for this and a time for that you are not always going to be worrying, always going to be happy, always going to be sad, always going to be celebrating but there's a time for each of these things in your life.

Ecclesiastes 3:1-8, A Time for Everything

"For everything there is a season, a time for every activity under heaven.

A time to be born and a time to die. A time to plant and a time to harvest.

A time to kill and a time to heal. A time to tear down and a time to build up.

A time to cry and a time to laugh. A time to grieve and a time to dance.

A time to scatter stones and a time to gather stones. A time to embrace and a time to turn away. A time to search and a time to quit searching. A time to keep and a time to throw away. A time to tear and a time to mend. A time to be quiet and a time to speak.

A time to love and a time to hate. A time for war and a time for peace."

It's important to not get stuck on one event or emotion, to move forward as it says in

Matthew 6:33 "*Seek first the kingdom of God and God's righteousness and all these things will be added unto you.*" Our focus sometimes is on everyone and everything around us rather than us as it says in

Matthew 7: 3-4 "*And why worry about a speck in your friend's eye when you have a log in your own? How can you think of saying to your friend, 'Let me help you get rid of that speck in your eye,' when you can't see past the log in your own eye?*"

Another words, how can we see clearly when our focus is on the wrong things. That will get us nowhere real fast. Can you relate to this? I know I can! I'm always focusing on my husband's flaws rather than mine. God's always telling me love more, patience more, compassion more!

> **John 14:6** Jesus said: "*I am the way, the truth and the life. No one can get to the Father, except through me.*" That's what are ministry is about spreading the
>
> Good News that Jesus Christ is life! Jesus is truth and Jesus is the only way to God the Father!

Victorious Living through Jesus!

"For whatever is born of God overcomes the world. And this is the victory that has overcome the world--our faith. Who is he who overcomes the world, but he who believes that Jesus is the Son of God?" 1 John 5:4-5

What is a great scripture that defines victorious living as it is written in the word of God, through Jesus Christ?

Psalm 105:1-4 *"Give thanks to the Lord and proclaim his greatness. Let the whole world know what he has done. Sing to him; yes, sing his praises. Tell everyone about his wonderful deeds. Exult in his holy name; rejoice, you who worship the Lord. Search for the Lord and for his strength; continually seek him."*

Isn't this a great daily guideline and standards for how we are to be in mind and with each other? Now in the same Psalm a very special servant of God is talked about:

Psalm 105:15, 17-19 *"Do not touch my chosen people, and do not hurt my prophets."*

"Then he sent someone to Egypt ahead of them--Joseph, who was sold as a slave. They bruised his feet with fetters and placed his neck in an iron collar. Until the time came to fulfill his dreams, the Lord tested Joseph's character."

So as it says there the Lord tested Joseph's character. Has your character been tested lately? If not than you better ask God to use you so that you can grow. You don't want to be sitting still and not being used. There's no blessings and no prosperity in that way of living or thinking. You've got to get up and do something or better yet let God do something with you and through you. He can and will if you will ask Him to. Let's read some scriptures on how we are to be in accord to the Kingdom of Heaven.

Matthew 5:19 *"So if you ignore the least commandment and teach others to do the same, you will be called the least in the Kingdom of Heaven. But anyone who obeys God's laws and teaches them will be called great in the Kingdom of Heaven."*

Matthew 19:30 *"But many who are the greatest now will be the least important then, and those who seem least important now will be the greatest then."*

Matthew 20:16 *"So those who are last now will be first then, and those who are first will be last."*

A great story in the bible of how one who has the favor of God starts out the very least, scum of the earth and end's up at the very most of authority and that story is about Joseph. Now let's read about this amazing conguest from Prison to Leadership and great authority all by and through the blessings and favor of God.

pt. 1 Genesis 39: 2-5 Joseph's Favor

pt. 2 Genesis 39:6-12 Temptation

pt. 3 Genesis 41:37-40 Joseph's Promotion

Enjoying Life with Jesus!

"And above all things have fervent love for one another, for "love will cover a multitude of sins." 1 Peter 4:8

What does it mean to enjoy? In the dictionary it is defined as to receive pleasure from; to take joy in or satisfaction. What is the definition for joy in the dictionary? A deep feeling or condition of happiness or contentment. We also see the word joy in the bible as to rejoice. Psalm 97:11-12, Psalm 118:24. Joy is the way we feel inside. This joy comes from our, *"faith expressing itself in love."* Galatians 5:6 It is the most wonderful natural high that we can experience from obedience in the Lord's will for our lives.

"For you have been called to live in freedom, my brothers and sisters. But don't use your freedom to satisfy your sinful nature. Instead, use your freedom to serve one another in love. For the whole law can be summed up in this one command: 'Love your neighbor as yourself.' But if you are always biting and devouring one another, watch out! Beware of destroying one another." Galatians 5:13-15

We will not enjoy our lives with Jesus if we are not loving like Jesus. This takes a lot of discipline and hanging out and spending time in God's word and in prayer and contemplation on the Word of God. What better use of your time right now than to do this? There is none; if you truly want a better life on the outside of this place. I tell you this from my personal experience. Even if you know all the scriptures, but you are not fulfilled inside and seeking other pleasures from the world; you will be lost and get back into all the things that got you where you are now. I did it, until I got into a good spirit-filled church and you will to. Be thinking about these things now, so that you will be better prepared when you get out of prison; to live a free life with Jesus. I love you and He loves us all so much! Don't take this most valuable time for granted. Please! If you do not already have parole plans or a safe place to go, then ask for help. I will use what resources and contacts I have to help you find good shelter and rehabilitation; to break the cycle of oppression right here.

"So I say let the Holy Spirit guide your lives. Then you won't be doing what your sinful nature craves. The sinful nature wants to do evil, which is just the opposite of what the Spirit wants. And the Spirit gives us desires that are the opposite of what the sinful nature desires. These two forces are constantly fighting each other, so you are not free to carry out your good intentions. But when you are directed by the Spirit, you are not under obligations to the law of Moses." Galatians 5:16-18

If you have never been filled with the Holy Spirit then say this prayer right now: "Father God, I repent of my sins, I humble myself before your throne. I am at your feet. I need your help. I want to do what is right and good. Please, make me a new person and fill me with your Holy Spirit. I invite the Holy Spirit into your temple, me; your creation, your daughter and/or son. I am ready to live for you. I know that I am not perfect and you will love me no matter what; but I want to live right and produce the fruits of the spirit, by my right living. I ask for your wisdom and guidance and will. I receive the Holy Spirit right now and I ask for the gift of speaking in tongues right now and discernment of spirits and prophetic utterances so that I may be a blessing to others and a good witness of the joy of living with Jesus." AMEN

 I want you to experience all that God promises we can, through living for Him in the bible. The more you know the more you can grow!

"Joyful are people of integrity, who follow the instructions of the Lord. Joyful are those who obey his laws and search for him with all their hearts. They do not compromise with evil, and they walk only in his paths. You have charge us to keep your commandments carefully. Oh, that my actions would consistently reflect your decrees! Then I will not be ashamed when I compare my life with your commands. As I learn your righteous regulations, I will thank you by living as I should! I will obey your decrees. Please dont give up on me!" Psalm 119:1-8

15. AUTHOR'S TESTIMONY

I grew up in a small town in Texas in the country. My parents divorced when I was 12 years old. I had 2 younger sisters and we lived with my dad. He was rewarded custody of us. I remember that I was afraid of my dad growing up. He was physically abusive and an alcoholic with a terrible temper. Finally at 16 I went to live with my mom. I had an awful temper too and I began drinking when I was 14. My mom's second husband was also an alcoholic with a bad temper and he smoked marijuana and sold it. So we had strange men coming to our house at all hours. I isolated myself in my room, reading, or listening to music. I met a college guy and we moved to Las Vegas by the time I was 20. I dropped out of high school when I was 17 a year before graduating. Although I got my GED I didn't ever stay in college. I got married when I was 21 and lived in Las Vegas until a year after we divorced at 24. I moved to Austin, TX then and tried to make a life for myself,f but soon I was drinking heavily and decided to move to Berkeley,CA . There I was doing ok for a little while until some shocking family news sent me into dangerous territory. I moved from Berkeley to Oakland, CA with a guy I barely knew and come to find out later he was drugging me and taping videos of us together. I was very unstable at this point in my life. After the Christmas holiday visiting my family I decided to move back to Austin. I moved in with a guy I barely knew again and he was addicted to marijuana and younger woman.

I smoked it once or twice with him and decided I didn't like it but then I'd smoke it behind his back to just deal with him and my life. I eventually moved out and was working for a while as a massage therapist until my drug addiction took over after I smoked some weed laced with a white foreign substance; could have been crack. It really made me go crazy. I was living on the street for about 4-6 months. Dates and times really are hard to pin point I was so lost. Around new years of 2007 I decided to visit my family in Corsicana, TX and that's when I was arrested driving my mom's car. They pulled up my record which included burglary and arson.

I spent the next 27 months of my life locked up behind bars. I was transferred from Corsicana jail to Austin jail and then finally to Hobby Unit, Marlin, TX where I spent the majority of my time. During my stay there I met a woman named Sheri Horn. We were in Painting & Decorating class together. She began to witness to me about Jesus Christ and September 23rd, 2007 I accepted Jesus Christ into my heart as my personal Lord and Savior. I began to read the bible and pray. It wasn't until March 2008 that I started going to church and August 30th, 2008 that I was baptized. Before I left prison I was told that I would be an evangelist ministering the word of God to many people and God spoke to me about writing inmates when I got out of prison Words of Encouragement Newsletter. I was released from Hobby unit March 23rd, 2009 and started the newsletter May 2009 after I got settled in Corsicana, TX.

I was living with my mom for a little while and started going to college. I went to AA every day that I could. I also made many sinful choices during the first 4-5 months. I slept with some different men and contracted the herpes virus. Which I have been cured of in the name of Jesus after using the medicine my OBGYN gave me! They say there is no cure but I know that Jesus is the cure.

 I decided to go to a Christian Recovery Group called Celebrate Recovery and then I was invited to their church Calvary Worship Center. There I met so many great people and the Holy Spirit really began to work on me. I prayed for a Godly husband and God provided. I met my husband Joseph D. Fincher at Calvary Worship Center. We were friends for a few months and then we dated for a few months before we got married January 2010 and I had our first baby "J.J." Joseph Jr. July 19th, 2010. As you can tell by the dates we conceived J.J. before we were married. But, the whole time we were together God's hand was on us and working in us and He still is today. As I write this book we are planning on having our second baby God willing and our son J.J. will turn 1 years old this month of July 2011.

We are praying for God's hand to expand our prison ministry beyond reaching 100 inmates to 1000+ and I know that He will provide the connections and resources to do this in His perfect will and timing. This book is also a blessing to reach out to those who are in prison and struggling.

This is the first of many testimonial books that I hope to write with the guidance of God's Holy Spirit. God's will be done at the center of my life. His will is my life and my plans. My husband Joseph has just started a Celebrate Recovery program up at our home church of Calvary Worship Center which now that I think about it is quite interesting how I was introduced to CWC through the C.R. program and then they stopped the program for some time after I started going to CWC and now my husband is starting that program again. God's hand is sovereign. He works in and through our lives in ways that is like a sewer sewing an afghan; it is beautiful and intricately designed.

We don't always realize the way He weaves and connects things together until we are later contemplating on it or writing about it. Never limit God's Divinity. There's nothing too big for our God to handle and work out!

NOTES:

NOTES:

NOTES:

Kim Fincher Ministries
1813 Sycamore Ave
Corsicana, TX 75110

ABOUT THE AUTHOR

Kimberly B. Fincher is Director of J.K.F. Prison Ministry, whose monthly mailing list started out in 2009 reaching 20 inmates on Hobby Unit, Marlin, TX; where she served time. Now, with the support of her Pastor Gary Johnson of Calvary Worship Center and her husband Joseph D. Fincher they are reaching over 100 inmates in 11 states and it continues to grow. By God's divine hand she has connected with Mitzi Hall of Free Life Ministries who publishes a quarterly ministry newsletter reaching 5,000 inmates; in which she is a contributing writer and Beth Michael's of Christian Pen Pal's recently added her info to their monthly newsletter. This is her first self-published book. She continues to write Words of Encouragement with Matthew 6:33 as the foundational scripture of her ministry in hopes to make disciples out of ex-convicts showing them the love of Christ Jesus and the value of building a lasting relationship with God. She is blessed with a wonderful family and a beautiful baby boy Joseph E. Fincher and they are expecting their second baby in April 2012. They reside in Coriscana, TX and our members of Calvary Worship Center.

Made in the USA
Charleston, SC
30 March 2012